*Atoms from
the Suns of
Solitude*

Atoms from the Suns of Solitude

Carroll Blair

Aveon Publishing Company

ISBN: 978-1-936430-41-3

Library of Congress Control Number
2011907212

Aveon Publishing Co.
P.O. Box 380739
Cambridge, MA 02238-0739 USA

Also by Carroll Blair

*The solitary moments of a life are the
most harmonious with the universe,
for it is a Solitude of infinite solitudes,
holding the great distance, the great
silence, boundless throughout time,
and beyond time.*

*Aloneness is filled with space, with
possibility, is where the power to be
is realized, and the emancipation
of a life is achieved.*

*Ever are searches being made to
find The Way outside, when signs
are everywhere pointing away to
the true path, leading to the inside.*

*Not raised from without, but awakened
within is the dawn of enlightenment.*

*The inner light is to receive, to guide,
to teach, to open a life to truth and
wisdom that abides when that of the
fading departs, but to be of benefit,
a journey must first be made.*

There is external image, and internal reality.

From the inner world is where the true make-up of the outer can best be perceived.

What moves of the visible is ever on its way to oblivion . . . (until turning the mind to what death cannot claim, the truth cannot be seen).

*With understanding comes a quieting;
with quietude, a deeper understanding.*

*As a twilight to a thousand sunrises is
the power of speech to that of silence.*

*The inner journey begins in silence; the
inner work begins in silence; all that
creates inner depth and growth begins
(and continues) in silence.*

*To enter silence is to enter the womb
of creation.*

*Though each life is manifest of the
same source, new is the form of its
energy when released.*

*The head of a matchstick contains fire,
but if not ignited, it is not released.
A human life contains the spiritual
within, but if never open, dormant
does its light and power remain.*

*Musing, probing, searching, then, **direction**; finding one's course, going the path that takes one to the eternal treasure.*

Unlike earthly riches, the treasure of the spiritual must be mined individually in order to be received.

The journey is not a ship of many, but a venture of one, realized by one.

The outer world is available for exploration by all, though it is the path that no other can set upon that is fundamental to the transcendent of one's life.

Of vital interest to a growing enlightenment is the unexplored, and nothing has been less explored in the human experience than the spiritual of human-being.

The promise for human advance depends on the spiritual evolution of the individual.

15

As an eagle without a sky is a human spirit without a solitude.

The power to create and comprehend in substantive measure cannot be attained without frequent occasions of solitary reflection.

Solitude is not only conducive, but also essential to work of the most serious nature.

It is the solitary work that liberates a life from the darkness that veils the eternal light, granting the greatest freedom to be known.

Offered at the summit of freedom is the experience of Now through the conscious- ness of eternity.

An infant reaches above, stretching its hands to something more . . . from the beginning, the instinct to reach for what is more, yet through the inner journey comes the realization that the way upward, is inward.

*Of the most beautiful paths of Nature
are those forged by the hand [the work]
of Nature; the paths of humankind yielding
the most in spiritual innovation are those
forged and pioneered by venturers of
the transcendent.*

*In the spiritual there is always
the potential to go further than the
distance that has heretofore been
journeyed.*

*Short is human life by measure of
the infinite, but its reach may extend
to the infinite.*

*Inspiration is a solitary affair, born of
a solitary mind and heart, and nurtured
in the solitude of an evolving life.*

*Solitude cannot be anything but friend to
the creative spirit, for the very nature of
solitude is of the creative.*

*Space for oneself, and time to develop one's
gifts . . . these are the indispensables that
one who is serious about the transcendent
cannot do without.*

One may find nourishment in the fruits of others, but no inner fruit can be seeded from them.

In addition to good nutrition and exercise, a body needs time in the outdoors for the fresh air and sunlight that are essential if it is to grow healthy and strong. For the spirit to grow in health and strength much time must be devoted to the spiritualization of inner being.

In aloneness is where the power of a life comes into its own, spiritually speaking.

*By society, breadth may be added to a
life, but the creation of inner depth is
the domain of solitude.*

*As all must go to their death alone, so
all must go to the life that is theirs alone.*

*The more that is learned and experienced,
the more striking becomes the unspoken
message that the answers one seeks, the
guidance that is needed to find one's way
must come from within.*

*Nowhere can so many puzzles be solved,
can so much confusion be unravelled
and greater clarity be found than in the
enlightened solitude.*

*To break inwardly with the predominance
of societal influence is not to break with
"order," but to quest for higher order (first
needing to get past the barriers of finite
consciousness, consumed with desires
and ambitions of a world of the passing).*

*Detachment is the first spiritual achievement
of note, for without it the imperishable of
one's life cannot be known.*

*What is of the eternal is all that bears the
soul of truth.*

*Like snow beneath a tropical sun goes all
production of the temporal.*

*As the ocean could not be explored without
a vessel, so one could not explore the eternal
without the vessel of one's temporal life
(though this vessel as good as docked for
a lifetime if not used to explore what time
cannot take away).*

Not by a fraction can the human experience be known without knowing the spiritual of human life.

The mind, heart and spirit hold the trinity of transcendence.

The more importance one gives to the passing moment, the further one is from engaging the Eternal Moment.

There is nothing that can be let go of in the temporal that is not the letting go of an illusion.

What is fleeting is by definition, of the trivial.

Earthly desires are exhaustible; not so, spiritual wonderment.

25

More wisdom is there in a child's search for hidden treasure than in the pursuit of false treasures of the fleeting.

Void of decoration is the spiritual, free of all but its essence.

The worldly is as rife with seduction as it is poor in substance.

*A life elevates by no other means than
what rises from within.*

*The greater the inner depth, the higher
its reach.*

*What one has, what one **is**, depends on
the measure of one's inner strength.*

One triumphs over what is walked away from only when it is transcended.

Ties must often be broken to ground one's life in what can never be broken.

One is willing to "play the game," to go along with farce only when the goal that one is after is less than noble.

To be free is not to be without cares,
but to be free of anxieties that derive
from an inordinate concern for affairs
of the fleeting.

The enlightened state is somewhat as the
universe in that it possesses much, but
doesn't strive to possess.

The vision of one preoccupied with minute
details of temporal life is like a man nearly
blind, his face close to a page trying to make
out the words with a magnifying glass. One
whose gaze is on the eternal, like someone
peering into the depths of the cosmos
through a large telescope.

There are people in regard to the potential of their lives who behave like someone pacing back and forth outside of his home, never going inside.

Spiritual power is ever present, but its access is not effortless — one doesn't become wise or virtuous simply by growing older — inner work, inner growth must there be to benefit from this privilege accorded to human life.

If someone never studied a foreign language no one would be surprised that, even at an elderly age, he would have no knowledge or skill of speaking it. Should it be wondered, then, if someone has never seriously engaged in inner work, that no sign of spiritual growth will (at any age) be in evidence?

Solitude to some is like a friend who one takes to immediately, the enjoyment of his or her company augmenting the more he or she is known and appreciated for what can be learned from them. To others, like the future friend who is feared at first, but gradually becoming a companion one grows to love and respect, also realizing the benefits the relationship can bring to one's life.

To draw the most from one's life (and more importantly, to give one's most to Life) requires time of withdrawal from the world.

Greater than the return of any monetary investment is the yield of time invested in a progressive solitude.

When the spiritual is awakened within,
one no longer looks to the outside for one's
salvation or paradise, for what is true and
always is also there, inside one, to guide
and bless with joys of inspiration.

Until reaching the ocean, the river is con-
fined to a comparatively narrow groove.
Until joining to the divine source, conscious-
ness remains narrow, confined to matters
of the finite world.

To go to the eternal is not to go to a place
of final rest, but to an inner world rich in
spiritual power and bliss.

It is ultimately not about one's relation to others, but one's connection to the eternal, able to give the most to one (and one, to give to others).

The highest wisdom, the deepest love of a life is realized where no outer eye can see.

In silence one nears closer to union with truth than by the teaching of any seer or sage.

Those dependent on others for the spiritual direction of their lives are as far from their spiritual power as the extent of their dependence.

From folly to folly they go who live all their days outside themselves.

To take Life with the seriousness it warrants and deserves, the day-to-day cannot be taken too seriously.

A symptom of spiritual infirmity is conformity to the fleeting.

Despite its conflicts the everyday world is one of pacification, for it has a tranquilizing effect on its participants, providing much surface activity to keep them occupied, but also keeping them from engaging with Life.

"What is it in our time that has significance for all time?" . . . A question too few of each generation ever ask themselves.

The best of what is available to human life is like having a priceless stone that is given at birth that many trade for a pittance soon after adopting the "go along to get along" ways of society.

To turn one's life over to the worldly is to give one's life to constant compromise of what should never be comprised.

One can as easily get used to darkness as one can to light.

Before giving their lives to anything the wise give their minds to thought and their hearts to love.

Things of the temporal matter to one, or are magnified in importance only because of ego.

What is widespread in popular culture is generally paper thin in significance.

How wise can obsession with the news of the moment be when the moment itself pays it no more attention than a meadow pays to a blade of grass that has blown away.

The great example of why nothing of the material should be clung to is in the material itself, shown by its eventual demise — that the destiny of everything of its kind is dissolution.

To seek out the good that doesn't fade, unfettered by the winds of the day is to remain ever close to the heart of truth.

Fads are attuned to the comings and goings of mediocrity, but not to the excellence of the indestructible.

One must sometimes stretch one's mind to grasp the profundity of Life that offers itself in every moment amid the swarm of trivialities vying for one's attention, as one would need to stretch one's ears to hear a theme of a magnificent symphony being played amid the clash of a dozen marching bands.

What is false cannot bear scrutiny of the unshadowed space of silence.

The further removed from illusion the clearer it is perceived.

The temporal world is full of groundless certainties, and nothing is of greater hindrance than this to spiritual growth.

As velocity and gravity together create the illusion that one is standing still on the earth, but is going round at tremendous speed, so is there an opposite illusion not uncommon among those who've yet to begin the inner journey, have yet to start living through the spiritual of their lives, though assuming themselves to be spiritually moving forward.

*A sense of reverence cannot be achieved in
preoccupation with what is not connected
to the transcendent.*

*The temporal has reign over the body,
not over the mind and spirit (unless it is
allowed to so reign).*

*To hold to even one manifest of the
dying is to not be near to freedom.*

Most of what makes living more difficult than it needs to be is (ironically) what humankind could most easily do without.

The enlightened choose carefully what they invite into their lives, and what invitations to accept from the outside.

In a natural setting an enlightened inner state will be in harmony with the external surroundings; in an artificially induced environment, it will be discordant.

Every moment of a spiritually oriented solitude is worth more than countless moments in company of a surface-based society.

All are involved in the business of keeping their lives going, but how many seriously ask themselves what they are doing, and where are they going?"

Regression is the inevitable course when not on the path that cultivates the better attributes of human life.

What is not of a spiritual character can be nothing but antagonistic to the fostering of higher principles.

Some feel they have to justify their lives to others, while others work toward creating a life of higher purpose in homage to Life.

To those who live by the fashions of society it is not what they are that matters, but what people think they are. For those who live apart from this, it is the reverse.

With increasing exposure to earthly ambitions one comes to realize if turned to what is greater, how much more is needed to live a noble life (and how much the pursuit of the meaningless interferes with achieving it).

Success that is based in the temporal can only be of the temporal.

Because someone or something has been recorded in a history book doesn't mean by this alone that the person, or subject in question, or reason for the recording was not of an ephemeral character.

Some have lived to chase after glory.
Others, to get to the miracle.

Eternal wisdom is the fruit of all seasons.

Even what lies well beneath the surface of
the earth lies not beneath the surface of life.

*To have lived wisely is to have engaged
time with spiritual purpose.*

*Progress of the worldly is but a shadow
of what human progress could be.*

*By rays of the material one may look,
but without the light of the spiritual
one cannot see.*

*Beyond the rank of leadership of anything
that is ego-driven is the honor of service
to the eternal.*

*Enlightenment is nowhere present where
what is being done is not in service of
its source.*

*Much of what goes on outside the spiritual
is of frivolity, banality, pretense, as empty
as the air surrounding its airs.*

The worldly places a high value on cleverness, though backs away from the truly profound.

Only what is real lives up to appearance.

The enlightened do not look to the popular of their age as a final standard for what is noble and worthy, but to the best of all ages combined, and there, render their highest respect.

What is a billion dollars made and squandered in the materialized world of commerce compared to one immortal work?

Where there is no excellence there is no joy beyond the ephemeral.

Achievement for earthly benefit alone falls short of contribution to Life.

The more one wants from the worldly, the more is one required to participate in systems of activity that are fundamentally corrupt. (A debasement of one's life for what soon fades away).

No matter how much or how often it is tried, there are two roads that can never be aligned in compromise: one leads to the selling of souls; the other, to their salvation.

What a life produces speaks to where it has been.

*Character operating through the better
nature prompts the mind to go further
in its quest for deeper wisdom.*

*As selfless as what is behind the universe's
creation is the higher nature, not needing
the applause of an audience for incentive
to perform.*

*Those who root their lives in the spiritual
learn of themselves, get to know themselves,
but then forget about themselves, turning their
attention to what is greater than themselves.*

As one brings Life into focus, clarity is brought to one's life.

To find wholeness life must be lived through the eternal, for only the eternal is complete.

How small does everything of the dying appear when reflecting on its mortality.

*In the temporal some things rise, though all
things set. Should not the most attention be
given to what never sets?*

*Imagine that someone is standing in the middle
of a large warehouse. On one side there is a
door opening from the bottom; on the opposite
side a door is closing from the top. Which way
to go . . . the door that is opening signifies the
conventional path of worldly ambition and the
pursuit of the material, centered in the temporal.
The door closing is the way to the spiritual, the
path to wisdom and light. This closing signify-
ing that for enlightenment to be attained and
profoundly benefit a life, the journey cannot be
started too late —one has only so much time
to spend on the trivial before coming to one's
(spiritual) senses and realizing what is good
and true, and worthy of giving a life to.*

*The other side is the spiritual side —in
this life.*

To go beyond one must leave behind.

*The greater the distance one moves from
the theater of the passing, the deeper the
realization that nothing could be more
right for the evolution of one's life.*

*How can one grow through inner light
if one is not freed from what prevents
its release?*

Of the finer gifts the outer world cannot give, for their provenance is within.

Ever moving toward greater light, greater love, greater being, is the spiritual work.

*The inner journey is **the** journey of a human life, for no hope can there be for transcendence until it begins.*

The kingdom is entered one at a time, by the
always solo journey to what is beyond time.

Lives may be lived on the surface of humanity,
*but there no **life** can be found.*

All are of now, though not all are in Now,
because all have not awakened to the eternal
of their lives.

*Depth cannot be in the life that doesn't
stay long enough in the spiritual work
to create it.*

*As there are laws of the physical universe,
so are there metaphysical laws of the
spiritual.*

*If one stays focused on the inner path
power beyond the temporal will be
revealed.*

*Until noble purpose has been established
internally, futile is the search for meaning.*

*Substantive growth cannot be generated from
a life's experience before connecting to what
is more than the experience.*

*The eternal is awakened to, but first it must
be labored to.*

*When engaged in work toward the transcendent
one is removed from the myriad of goings-on
that can distract and entice one away from the
most important work that can be engaged.*

*Some fail to go higher, deeper, further, out of
fear they will no longer be "seen" by others,
but to go into a spiritual distance is to not
have concern for such things, for the ego
is discarded along the way.*

*It is only when on one's own mentally and
emotionally that the spiritualization of a life
is achievable.*

The great space is in solitude, there for the great task.

An unfoldment, not an instant attainment is liberation, realized through an unwavering commitment to the spiritual path.

To grow in spirituality is to change, drawing from the force of the never changing.

When opening to the demands of the higher path one cannot feel that one's time is being ill-spent. Can the same be said when catering to demands of a worldly nature?

To seek to be more without obsession with wanting more is principal to spiritual development.

There is room for error on the spiritual journey, but not insincerity.

*In aloneness is where the answer can be
known to how serious one is about doing
what is necessary to reach the higher
dimension of human-being.*

*Nothing that generates from the temporal
can pave the way or pay the price for a
spiritual awakening.*

*Until free of all interests to impress, one is
not prepared for union with the infinite.*

*Not a retreat into self is the spiritual solitude,
but a journey to where the deepest connection
to the soul of Life can be made.*

*Through forgetfulness of the world of ego
a timeless remembrance of truth and divine
love lies open to the spirit of light.*

*When on the right path one can be alone,
though not be lonely. When on the wrong
path one can be in company of all kinds,
and feel loneliness.*

A growing wisdom calms. A growing ambition troubles when baseness is the way of its character.

If the daylight of the world were to suddenly go dark, the state of those living through the inner light would not be disturbed.

The spirit of enlightenment is of a faceless beauty . . . like a river, but beneath its waters; like a mountain, but inside its rock.

A spiritual sentience is one that understands beyond the word, the sight, the sound, the touch.

There is much to learn from contemplation of the world's perpetual turn.

What the perfect ambiance is to a shared moment of friendship is what the ambiance of solitude is to the contemplative mind.

There are times of solitary rumination
imbued by the spiritual where inspiration
is directed in a continuous flow of insight
accompanied by the deepest sense of peace.

One cannot leave a footprint on the water,
a handprint on the wind, yet a foot, a hand
is placed upon it, though without evidence
it was there. The same with the mysteries
of mind and spirit — of a source recognized
in manifest, but itself, invisible, untraceable,
without tangible evidence that it exists.

When opening to the unknown good things
soon present themselves at the opening,
like welcoming someone home.

*The eternal is unmoved by all promptings
of the senses fixated on the temporal.*

Eternity Is. Time is ever moving into was.

*Stillness is as a mirror on which the eternal
bears its reflection.*

Until the inner quieting, a human life cannot know the range of its gifts.

It is to silence that the human spirit owes its greatest debt.

The quiet moment is pregnant with insight and vision of a depth and scope like no other setting.

*In every moment silence is somewhere
giving birth to the wondrous.*

*When the mind is enlightened it does
not seek for joys, for joys then come
to the mind.*

*As the mind is most effective when it is
calm, so is the heart.*

Bliss . . . like the Morning of mornings,
holding a billion suns.

An experience of no greater intensity is
there than that of the enlightened calm.

In the elevated calm the fury is understood.

The spiritual does not take nourishment from the worldly; the worldly has not the means to digest the spiritual.

The great power is from that which has no interest in what anything of the worldly would refer to as power.

To covet nothing of the temporal is to remain close to the eternal.

*They live freely who go without fear of
what could happen at any time, living
without holding on.*

*A human life is born with barriers
that must be removed if it is to be born
unto Life.*

*One can have everything that means
something wherever one may be if
realized that part of one is also of
eternity, untouched by place and time.*

*One enters the world as a dying being
to experience if one wills, the Great Undying.*

*The spiritual holds the key; the earthly,
only locks.*

*They bring nothing but dust to their return
to dust who have lived solely for that of
the passing.*

The best of the worldly is as a leaf wafting past the fruit of the eternal.

What comes to nothing was nothing from the start.

Ever hungry is the lower nature (the animality of human character), and always wanting what is counter to the spiritual advancement of humankind.

*Little is needed of all that man pursues,
the lower nature spurring those on whose
lives it directs to the gratification of want
after needless want.*

*Greater than the strength to greedily
amass, to dominate, to conquer, is
conquering the lust for such endeavor.*

*The noble motive is something that one
serves. The base, something to which
one is enslaved.*

From one's beginning, the selfishness of human animality is awake. The spiritual needs to be awakened.

Selfless thought, selfless feeling precedes selfless offering.

The more satisfied with materiality for the basis of life, the more distant is one from guidance of the inner light.

*Of profound moment is the dawn of clarity
of what is relevant and irrelevant to living
a substantive life (which must always be
of service to the goal of contribution).*

*As impartial in its giving as is the earth
of its bounty is the life transcendent.*

*In union with the source of eternal being
does the higher impulse bestir one to be.*

*To live through the lower nature is to be
without introspection, and by its absence
no conscious connection to Life can
be achieved.*

*The journey to the promised land is the inner
journey from the animal to the spiritual
of human-being.*

*The path is of the work; the work is of the
path.*

*The noble of spirit never feel they do not
have enough, though not foreign is the
feeling of not having grown enough,
or given enough.*

*Enlightenment is present in appreciation,
though not in a soliciting for appreciation
from others.*

*There is no such thing as a "grand" ambition
when the ambition is of a worldly character.*

The higher nature seeks only to serve the sublime.

Of the great possessions is the freedom from all yearning for possession.

Where there is attachment, love cannot be present.

No great heart is full of wants.

There is a world of difference between attachment and devotion.

Many have given much for perceived treasures of the outer world, but nothing of time and effort to find the greatest of treasure that is their own.

*Forward does human life go in the
spiritual to the degree that it is willing
to let go.*

*On the journey to light, one learns to live
with strength and courage and appreciate
the privileged ways of selflessness.*

*To be granted a chance for a life of spiritual
realization is profoundly blessful as well as
blissful.*

It is not possible to know all, but it is to experience something of the power of All.

An experience of a lifetime do many long for, when they could have the experience of an eternity if willing to pay the price.

The surrendering of I [of ego] is required when entering into the infinite, the return being access to the partaking of what nothing of the transitory can enter.

Not "self-improvement," but spiritual
maturity is the goal of transcendence.

As a shallow pond to a mighty ocean is the
stature of self alone to that of the spiritual.

Through higher conduct one gets to what
is whole and true.

*The further removed from inner dependence
on the temporal the clearer the distinction
is perceived between the real and the unreal.*

*Falsehood comes in and out of being. Truth
is ever in Being.*

Of make-believe is the world of the fleeting.

*An advance in the worldly is the reverse
in the spiritual.*

*As a life on earth cannot survive in its
natural state beyond the atmosphere
of its skies, so ego, being solely of the
temporal, cannot exist in the realm
of the eternal.*

*Only when rooted in the immutable is
ascension of human life possible.*

*When the lower nature is transcended,
the point of concentration then turns to
the challenge of spiritual ascendancy.*

*If one were given the full spectrum of
spiritual gifts at once without the trials
of the journey, much that is invaluable
to the process of growth would not be
learned and received.*

*A life of progressive growth is one of
focus and attention to the unfolding
of its purpose.*

Who has the fewest wants also has the fewest needs outside of what the body requires, but they are the maturest of needs, and of the higher nature.

In transcendence there is a love beyond sentimentality; a generosity beyond the offerings of self-interest; a stoic calm that is the opposite of coolness or indifference; a detachment filled with sensitivity and awareness, strength and benevolence, living a spiritual depth unknown to one who keeps to the surface of his life.

Freedom has ultimately to do with what is going on within, not with external mobility, or what one is able to do in the outer world.

Without focus freedom is nothing, and focus is not possible without discipline.

Discipline doesn't restrict, but expands the freedom of a life.

The temporal is rife with nonessentials, the avoidance of many being compulsory if the higher responsibilities are to be successfully met.

Spiritual growth transpires on its own time, but doesn't happen if the work required is left undone.

The discipline that elevates endures by grace of the humble heart.

When humility is at the summit of achievement it looks not down, but up to see how much more there is to be done.

What is raised by ego inevitably falls to barren ground.

What no one can do for another is the work that will bring forth the best of what one can contribute to the world.

An item of fruit doesn't complete its function until all of its juice and fiber has been consumed. A human life, until it has given all it has to give.

*The heart of love is won when the heart
for glory is lost.*

*Nothing is quieter or less assuming than
true devotion (its essence being of the
selfless, in union with the higher nature).*

*Of more significance to the advance
of the journey than what is learned
from others is what no one can learn
from anyone.*

Spiritually speaking one gains more when walking alone than when running with the herd.

For the devoted aspirant esteem and honor are of no importance, whether he or she has them or not.

It is not they who are of inner luminosity who are interested in outshining others.

*Only ego works to be celebrated; to be
at every banquet in celebration of itself.*

*A life cannot operate with vision beyond
the temporal until waking to the higher
path.*

*Greater the privilege to be born into
the spiritual than to be born into worldly
wealth.*

*It is when joined to the eternal in devoted
service that a human life has the agency
to transform, the power to truly grow.*

*No more can one access spiritual treasure
without inner work than one can stand
before a mine of the earth and summon
its metal to the surface.*

*It is in aloneness where the spirit is
best forged and strengthened for the
challenges of higher growth.*

*Though not always producing, the spiritual
solitude is ever at work.*

*To have a mind and spirit to oneself is to
have a universe to oneself, but with growing
awareness comes the realization that the gifts
of this universe are not for one to keep.*

*Ones who live through ego set out to make
their mark in the world; who live through
the spiritual, to create their contribution —
(sometimes in retirement from the world).*

Spiritual detachment is something of a withdrawal, but extends to its measure in open generosity and love.

It is they who have found the eternal of their lives who live an eternal gratitude.

Through all shades of mind and heart the presence of gratitude remains in the enlightened spirit.

Those who bring their lives to Life receive its abundance of blessings (among them the richest blessings that can be granted to human life).

The louder the world becomes, the weaker the connection to the higher instinct to move humanity to what is more than the noise and masquerade of the fleeting.

For many, the greater unknown is not without, but within.

Each must find his own way out of the false and the base; her own way into the authentic and the profound.

As the earth's sun is without satellites, so the enlightened of spirit seek no satellites, but encourage all who draw near to them to find their way to their inner sun and give to the world its light.

Who remains the disciple of another remains lost.

*The spiritual wealth of one is not to be
idolized, but to be an inspiration for others
to go in search of their own.*

*Greater than the successes of earthly
ambitions is a devotion to the exploration
of human spiritual potential.*

*If always available for the temporalities
of the day, of what service can one be to
what is true and everlasting?*

The spiritual is infinite, though can imbue a life only to the degree that it opens to all that is being offered.

Before fading the flower wholly opens to its star.

Enlightenment surrenders nothing to the temporal and resists nothing from the eternal.

The highest sobriety is intoxication with the sublime.

Some leave a word to the tome of eternity; others, a sentence; others, a paragraph; and some leave nothing, because while they were living, they missed the eternal of their lives.

As much treasure as has been mined from the spiritual dimension of humankind, more is there to be discovered.

*No higher gift can human beings give
than to pass on the best of gifts that are
bequeathed to humanity, realized through
finding within what is void of ego, what
speaks to the universal, set forth in a variety
of manner and form to serve the hope for
a world of less ignorance than wisdom,
of more light than darkness, of less enmity
than love.*

*Dreams abound to explore the cosmos, which
now cannot be done, when an even greater
feat awaits, one within grasp of human life,
a challenge that beckons humanity to the
extraordinary; to possibilities that could
be turned to reality by virtue of an internal
power able to birth a freedom and peace to
allow for what nothing of a material world
could satisfy; a life to truly be made whole
through a sacred realm that has long been
neglected, ready to grace humanity, to
transform the most promising entity on earth
into a state of being that would aspire to create
a new world, rising to the acceptance of its
greater calling.*

ABOUT THE AUTHOR

Carroll Blair is an author of more than twenty books and the recipient of numerous awards. His work has been well endorsed and commendably reviewed. Among his titles cited for distinction are *Through the Shadows*, winner of the Pacific Book Awards, and Quarter *Notes*, winner of the Sharp Writ Book Awards. He is an alumnus of the Boston Conservatory and lives in Massachusetts.

www.ingramcontent.com/pod-product-compliance
Lightning Source LLC
Chambersburg PA
CBHW021203020426
42331CB00003B/181